DREAM
Explore
DISCOVER

summersdale

DREAM. EXPLORE. DISCOVER.

An Hachette UK Company
www.hachette.co.uk

Summersdale Publishers Ltd
Part of Octopus Publishing Group Limited
Carmelite House
50 Victoria Embankment
LONDON
EC4Y 0DZ
UK

www.summersdale.com

Printed and bound in China

ISBN: 978-1-78783-022-6

Substantial discounts on bulk quantities of Summersdale books are available to corporations, professional associations and other organizations. For details contact general enquiries: telephone: +44 (0) 1243 771107 or email: enquiries@summersdale.com.

TO...

FROM...

I WILL GO ANYWHERE,
PROVIDED IT BE

forward.

DAVID LIVINGSTONE

TWENTY YEARS FROM NOW YOU WILL BE MORE DISAPPOINTED BY THE THINGS THAT YOU DIDN'T DO THAN BY THE ONES YOU DID DO.

SARAH FRANCES BROWN

LET
ADVENTURES
FILL YOUR
SOUL

LIVE, TRAVEL, ADVENTURE, BLESS, AND DON'T BE SORRY.

JACK KEROUAC

I GO TO NATURE TO BE SOOTHED AND HEALED, AND TO HAVE MY SENSES PUT IN TUNE ONCE MORE.

John Burroughs

TRUST THE DREAMS,
FOR IN THEM IS
HIDDEN THE

gate to eternity.

Kahlil Gibran

LIFE IS A
HELLUVA LOT MORE
FUN IF YOU SAY "YES"
RATHER THAN "NO".

RICHARD BRANSON

**IF YOU OBEY
ALL THE RULES,
YOU MISS ALL
THE FUN.**

Katharine Hepburn

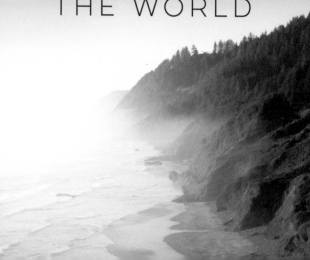

WANDERLUST:
n. A STRONG DESIRE TO WANDER, TRAVEL AND EXPLORE THE WORLD

THE PURPOSE OF
LIFE... IS TO LIVE
IT, TO TASTE
EXPERIENCE TO
THE UTMOST,
TO REACH OUT
EAGERLY AND
WITHOUT FEAR
FOR NEWER
AND RICHER
EXPERIENCE.

Eleanor Roosevelt

BE
WILD
AND
WONDER

EVERYTHING YOU'VE EVER WANTED IS ON THE OTHER SIDE OF

FEAR.

GEORGE ADDAIR

Either I will find a way, or I will make one.

PHILIP SIDNEY

The journey changes
you... It leaves marks
on your memory, on
your consciousness,
on your heart, and
on your body.

Anthony Bourdain

SAY
YES to
NEW ADVENTURES

Difficulties

ARE JUST
THINGS TO

overcome,

AFTER
ALL.

ERNEST SHACKLETON

EVERY MAN CAN

transform

THE WORLD FROM ONE OF
MONOTONY AND DRABNESS
TO ONE OF EXCITEMENT AND

adventure.

IRVING WALLACE

ERRANEE

Make
EVERY DAY
→
COUNT

LIVE IN THE
SUNSHINE,
SWIM THE SEA,
DRINK THE
WILD AIR'S
SALUBRITY.

Ralph Waldo Emerson

WHEN YOU PUT YOUR
HAND IN A FLOWING
STREAM, YOU TOUCH
THE LAST THAT HAS
GONE BEFORE AND
THE FIRST OF WHAT
IS STILL TO COME.

LEONARDO DA VINCI

A SHIP IN A HARBOUR IS SAFE – BUT THAT IS NOT WHAT SHIPS ARE BUILT FOR.

JOHN A. SHEDD

IT IS ADVISABLE

= TO LOOK =

FROM THE
TIDE POOL TO THE

STARS

⟩ AND ⟨

THEN BACK TO
THE TIDE POOL
AGAIN.

JOHN STEINBECK

Turn your face to the sun and the shadows fall behind you.

MĀORI PROVERB

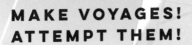

**MAKE VOYAGES!
ATTEMPT THEM!**

*There's
nothing else.*

Tennessee Williams

FOR MY PART, I TRAVEL
NOT TO GO ANYWHERE
BUT TO GO. I TRAVEL
FOR TRAVEL'S SAKE.

ROBERT LOUIS STEVENSON

IF YOU CAN FIND
A PATH WITH NO
OBSTACLES,
IT PROBABLY
DOESN'T LEAD

ANYWHERE.

FRANK A. CLARK

IN EVERY
CURVING BEACH,
IN EVERY GRAIN
OF SAND THERE
IS THE STORY
OF THE EARTH.

Rachel Carson

The mountains
are calling and
I must go.

John Muir

OPEN YOUR HEART
TO THE SKY.

Live.

ADAM GNADE

THE SUN
DOES NOT

shine

FOR A FEW TREES
AND FLOWERS,
BUT FOR THE

wide world's

JOY.

HENRY WARD BEECHER

NOT TILL WE
ARE LOST...
DO WE BEGIN

to find
ourselves.

Henry David Thoreau

THE BOLD ADVENTURER

succeeds

THE BEST.

OVID

IT IS ONLY IN

ADVENTURE

= THAT =

SOME PEOPLE
SUCCEED IN

≷ KNOWING ≷

THEMSELVES — IN

≷ FINDING ≷

THEMSELVES.

ANDRÉ GIDE

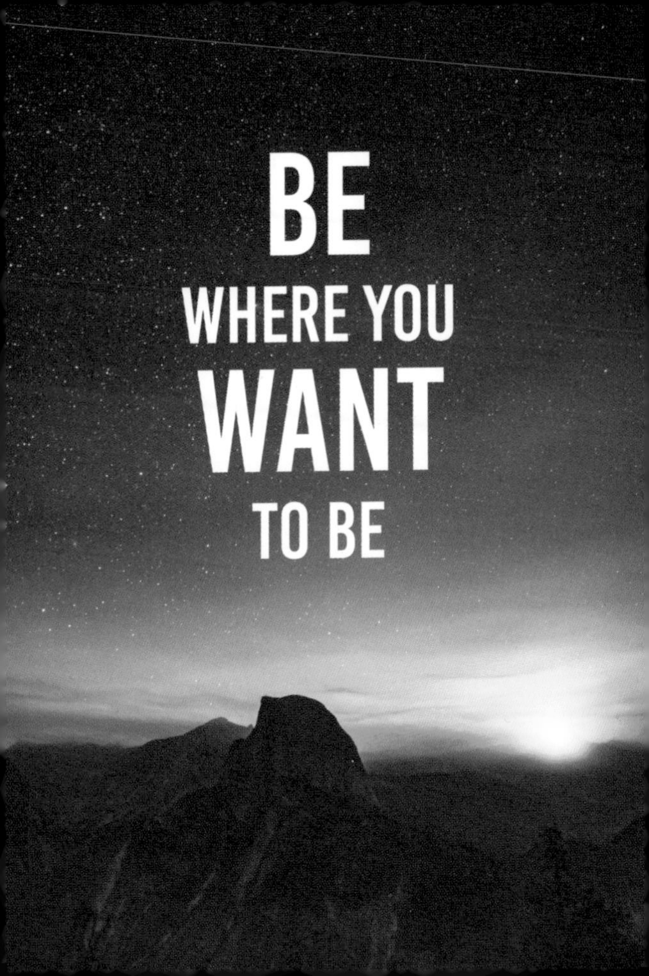
BE
WHERE YOU
WANT
TO BE

LIFE
IS EITHER
A DARING
ADVENTURE
or NOTHING.

HELEN KELLER

FORGET NOT THAT THE
EARTH DELIGHTS TO FEEL
YOUR BARE FEET AND
THE WINDS LONG TO
PLAY WITH YOUR HAIR.

KAHLIL GIBRAN

THE
BIG
QUESTION

IS WHETHER YOU ARE GOING TO BE ABLE TO SAY

A HEARTY YES TO YOUR ADVENTURE.

Joseph Campbell

COLLECT
MOMENTS,
NOT
THINGS

A JOURNEY IS *a person* IN ITSELF; NO TWO ARE ALIKE... WE DO NOT TAKE A TRIP; *a trip* TAKES US.

JOHN STEINBECK

I HAVEN'T BEEN EVERYWHERE, *but it's on my list.*

Susan Sontag

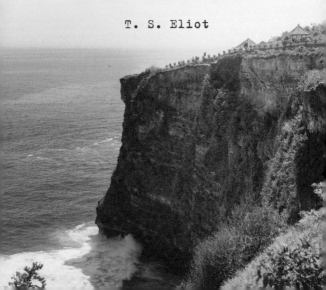

ONLY THOSE WHO WILL RISK GOING TOO FAR CAN POSSIBLY FIND OUT HOW FAR ONE CAN GO.

T. S. Eliot

WILDERNESS IS
NOT A LUXURY
BUT A NECESSITY
OF THE HUMAN
SPIRIT.

Edward Abbey

THE VERY BASIC CORE OF A MAN'S LIVING SPIRIT IS HIS PASSION FOR ADVENTURE.

CHRISTOPHER McCANDLESS

the greatest

ADVENTURES

LIE AHEAD

LIFE SHRINKS
OR EXPANDS IN
PROPORTION
TO ONE'S
COURAGE.

Anaïs Nin

You only get one chance at life and you have to grab it boldly.

BEAR GRYLLS

THE MAN WHO GOES
AFOOT, PREPARED TO
CAMP ANYWHERE AND
IN ANY WEATHER, IS
THE MOST INDEPENDENT
FELLOW ON EARTH.

HORACE KEPHART

BE LIKE
A RIVER.
BE OPEN.

FLOW.

JULIE CONNOR

One way to get the
most out of life
is to look upon it
as an adventure.

William Feather

DO A LITTLE
MORE EACH DAY

THAN YOU THINK
YOU POSSIBLY
CAN.

LOWELL THOMAS

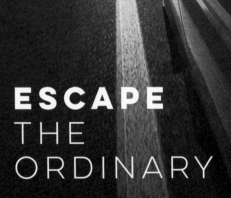

ESCAPE
THE
ORDINARY

OPTIMISM IS TRUE MORAL COURAGE.

ERNEST SHACKLETON

THE OCEAN
STIRS THE HEART,
INSPIRES THE
IMAGINATION AND
BRINGS ETERNAL
JOY TO THE SOUL.

Robert Wyland

TO AWAKEN QUITE ALONE
IN A STRANGE TOWN IS ONE
OF THE PLEASANTEST

sensations

IN THE WORLD.

FREYA STARK

Adventure is worthwhile in itself.

AMELIA EARHART

Follow
YOUR OWN
PATH

IF YOU COME
TO A FORK IN
THE ROAD,

take it!

Yogi Berra

BE FEARLESS
IN THE PURSUIT
OF WHAT SETS

your soul

ON FIRE.

JENNIFER LEE

Travel

IS THE ONLY
THING YOU BUY
THAT MAKES YOU

➤➤➤

RICHER

NATURE GIVES TO EVERY TIME AND SEASON SOME BEAUTIES OF ITS OWN.

CHARLES DICKENS

THERE IS NO
CERTAINTY;
THERE IS ONLY
ADVENTURE.

Roberto Assagioli

YOUR TIME IS LIMITED, SO DON'T WASTE IT LIVING SOMEONE ELSE'S LIFE.

STEVE JOBS

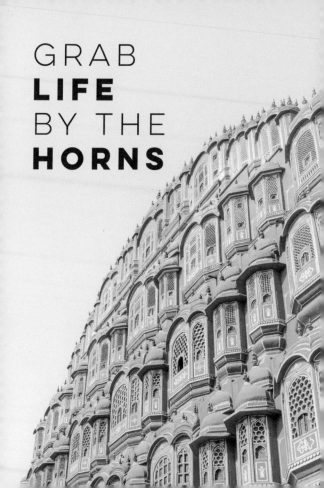

GRAB
LIFE
BY THE
HORNS

THE FUTURE
BELONGS TO
THOSE WHO
BELIEVE IN
THE BEAUTY OF
THEIR DREAMS.

Eleanor Roosevelt

IT IS IN THE
COMPELLING
= ZEST OF =
HIGH ADVENTURE
AND OF VICTORY,
> AND IN <
CREATIVE ACTION,
THAT MAN FINDS HIS
SUPREME JOYS.

ANTOINE DE SAINT-EXUPÉRY

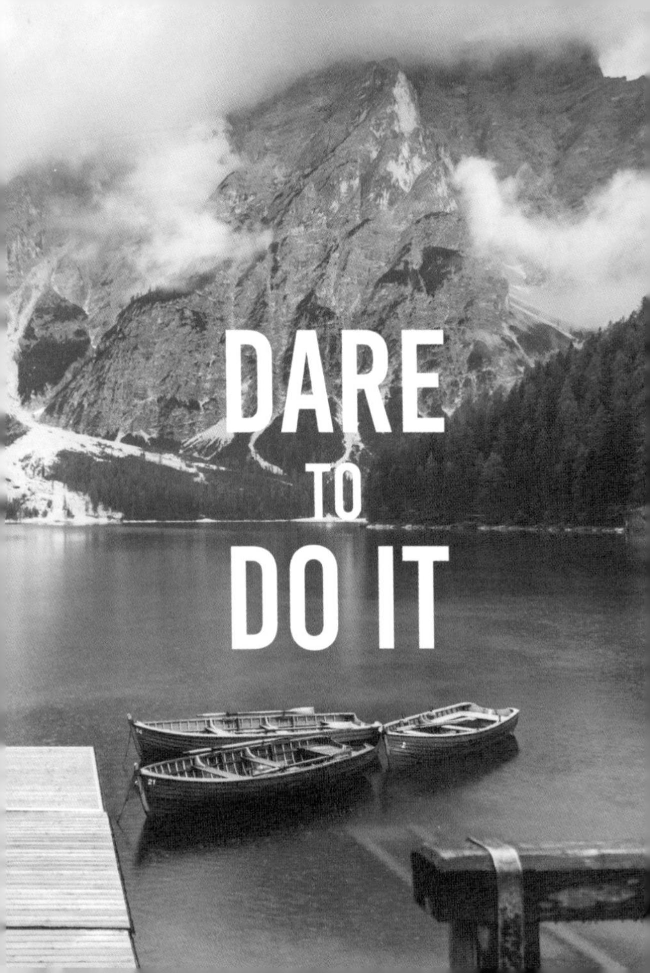
DARE
TO
DO IT

A RIVER IS MORE THAN AN AMENITY, IT IS A TREASURE.

OLIVER WENDELL HOLMES JR

IN THE PRESENCE
OF NATURE,
A WILD DELIGHT

RUNS THROUGH
THE MAN.

Ralph Waldo Emerson

THE ROUGHEST

roads

OFTEN LEAD TO THE TOP.

CHRISTINA AGUILERA

MAN
CANNOT DISCOVER
= NEW OCEANS =
UNLESS HE HAS
THE COURAGE
> TO <
LOSE SIGHT OF
THE SHORE.

ANDRÉ GIDE

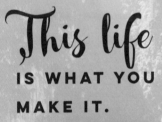

This life
IS WHAT YOU
MAKE IT.

Marilyn Monroe

A LAKE
CARRIES YOU
INTO RECESSES
OF FEELING
OTHERWISE
IMPENETRABLE.

William Wordsworth

Mountains
ARE THERE TO

⫸⫸⫸————————➤

BE CLIMBED

Today
IS A
>>>————————————>
BRAND
NEW DAY

A
ROLLING
STONE
GATHERS NO
MOSS.

ERASMUS

PEOPLE DO
NOT DECIDE
TO BECOME
EXTRAORDINARY.
THEY DECIDE
TO ACCOMPLISH
EXTRAORDINARY
THINGS.

Edmund Hillary

THERE IS NO INSTINCT LIKE THAT OF
the heart.

Lord Byron

GOOD
COMPANY
MAKES >THE> WAY
SEEM
SHORT.

IZAAK WALTON

THERE IS ALWAYS SOMETHING TO MAKE YOU WONDER IN THE SHAPE OF A TREE, THE TREMBLING OF A LEAF.

ALBERT SCHWEITZER

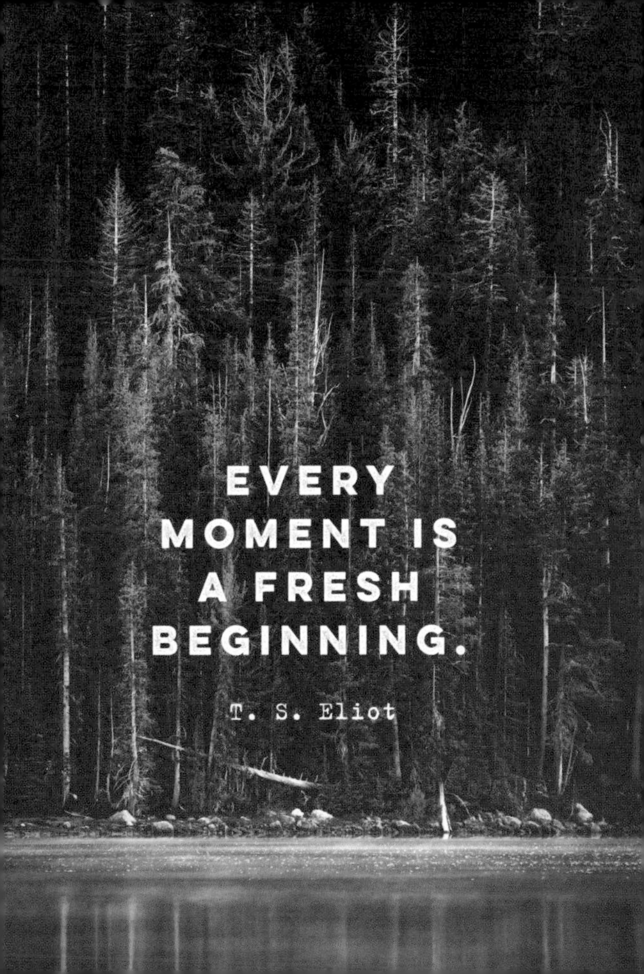
EVERY
MOMENT IS
A FRESH
BEGINNING.
T. S. Eliot

TELL ME, WHAT
IS IT YOU PLAN
TO DO WITH YOUR
ONE WILD AND

precious life?

Mary Oliver

GREAT THINGS ARE DONE WHEN MEN AND MOUNTAINS MEET.

WILLIAM BLAKE

WE
TRAVEL
= NOT TO =
ESCAPE LIFE,
BUT FOR
❯ LIFE ❮
NOT TO
ESCAPE US.

ANONYMOUS

LET'S
GET
LOST

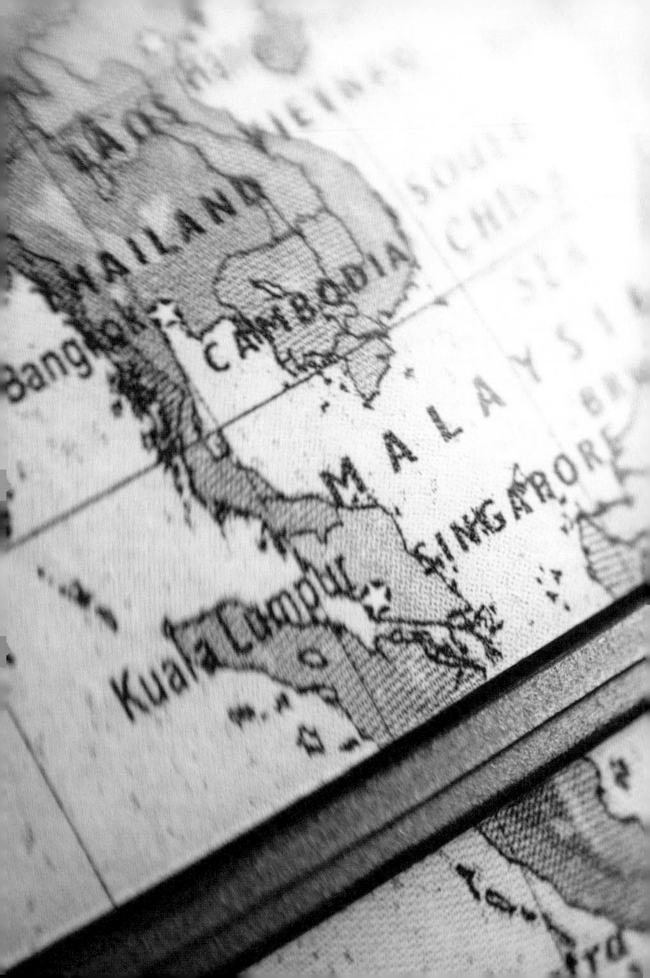
CAMBODIA
Bangkok
SINGAPORE
Kuala Lumpur

IT ISN'T WHERE
YOU CAME FROM.

IT'S **WHERE**
YOU'RE GOING
THAT COUNTS.

Ella Fitzgerald

IF
happiness
IS THE GOAL...
THEN
adventures
SHOULD BE
TOP PRIORITY.

RICHARD BRANSON

THE SEA IS AS NEAR AS WE COME TO ANOTHER WORLD.

ANNE STEVENSON

THE QUESTION
ISN'T WHO IS
GOING TO LET ME;
IT'S WHO IS
GOING TO

stop me.

Ayn Rand

OUR MEMORIES OF
THE OCEAN WILL LINGER
ON, LONG AFTER OUR
FOOTPRINTS IN THE
SAND ARE GONE.

ANONYMOUS

HOW INAPPROPRIATE TO CALL THIS PLANET EARTH WHEN IT IS CLEARLY OCEAN.

ARTHUR C. CLARKE

START WHERE
YOU ARE. USE
WHAT YOU
HAVE. DO WHAT
YOU CAN.

Arthur Ashe

Smooth seas do not make skillful sailors.

AFRICAN PROVERB

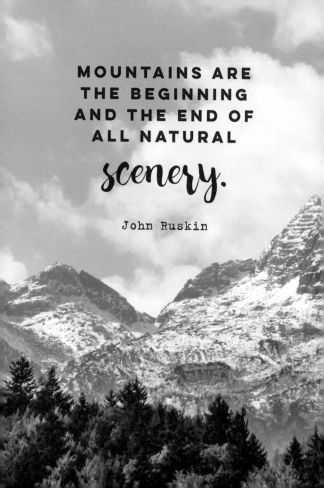

THAT
QUALITY
= OF AIR =

THAT EMANATES
FROM OLD TREES...
SO WONDERFULLY

≳ CHANGES ≲

AND RENEWS A
WEARY SPIRIT.

ROBERT LOUIS STEVENSON

THE

SIGHT OF THE
STARS

ALWAYS MAKES
ME **DREAM.**

VINCENT VAN GOGH

Find
YOUR WILD
SIDE

THERE IS NO END TO
THE ADVENTURES THAT
WE CAN HAVE IF ONLY
WE SEEK THEM WITH
OUR EYES OPEN.

JAWAHARLAL NEHRU

A JOURNEY

OF

A THOUSAND MILES

BEGINS WITH A

SINGLE

STEP.

LAO TZU

CLIMB THE
MOUNTAIN NOT
TO PLANT
YOUR FLAG,

BUT TO EMBRACE
THE CHALLENGE,
ENJOY THE AIR AND
BEHOLD THE VIEW.

CLIMB IT SO
YOU CAN SEE
THE WORLD.

David McCullough Jr

Life is

BETTER WHEN YOU

TRAVEL

THE EARTH HAS ITS MUSIC FOR THOSE WHO WILL LISTEN.

George Santayana

I'D RATHER
REGRET THE
THINGS I'VE DONE
THAN REGRET
THE THINGS I
HAVEN'T DONE.

Lucille Ball

LIFE IS A JOURNEY NOT A DESTINATION

IF THERE IS MAGIC ON THIS PLANET, IT IS CONTAINED IN WATER.

Loren Eiseley

A TRUE TRAVELLER HAS NO FIXED PLAN, AND IS NOT INTENT ON ARRIVING.

LAO TZU

THE ONLY PERSON YOU ARE DESTINED TO BECOME IS THE PERSON YOU DECIDE TO BE.

Ralph Waldo Emerson

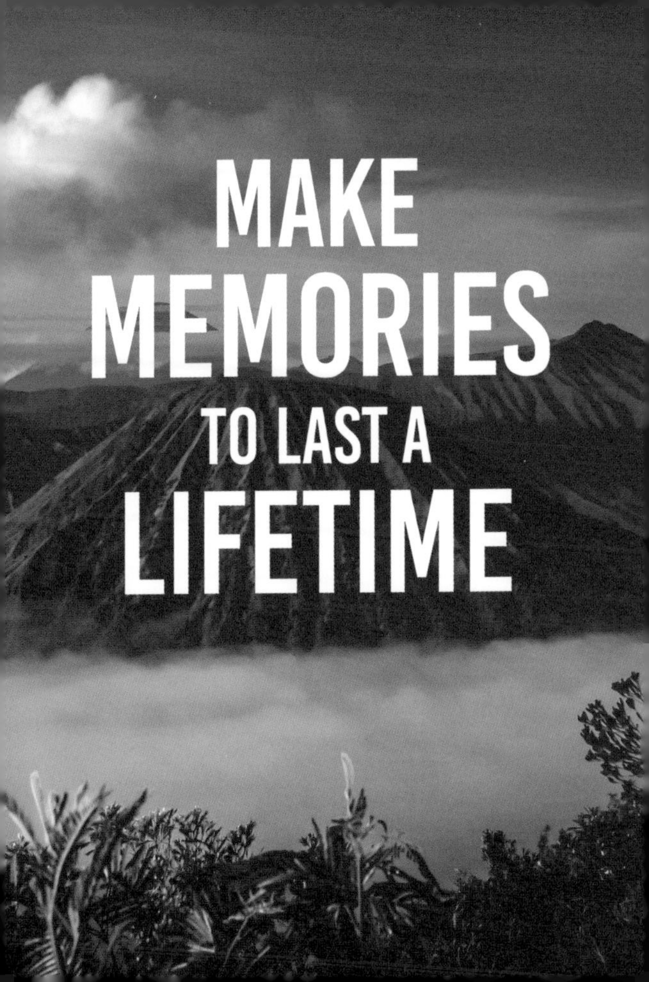
MAKE
MEMORIES
TO LAST A
LIFETIME

EARTH AND SKY, WOODS
AND FIELDS, LAKES AND
RIVERS, THE MOUNTAIN
AND THE SEA... TEACH
SOME OF US MORE
THAN WE CAN EVER
LEARN FROM BOOKS.

JOHN LUBBOCK

WHAT LIES BEHIND
US AND WHAT LIES
BEFORE US ARE
SMALL MATTERS
COMPARED TO
WHAT LIES

within us.

Henry S. Haskins

What you do today can improve all your tomorrows.

RALPH MARSTON

GREAT
THINGS
NEVER
COME FROM
COMFORT
ZONES

LOOK DEEP
INTO NATURE,
AND THEN YOU WILL

understand

EVERYTHING
BETTER.

ALBERT EINSTEIN

WE TRAVEL,
SOME OF US

forever,

TO SEEK OTHER

states,

OTHER LIVES,
OTHER SOULS.

ANAÏS NIN

PLUNGE BOLDLY INTO
THE THICK OF LIFE...
SEIZE IT WHERE YOU
WILL, IT IS ALWAYS
INTERESTING.

JOHANN WOLFGANG VON GOETHE

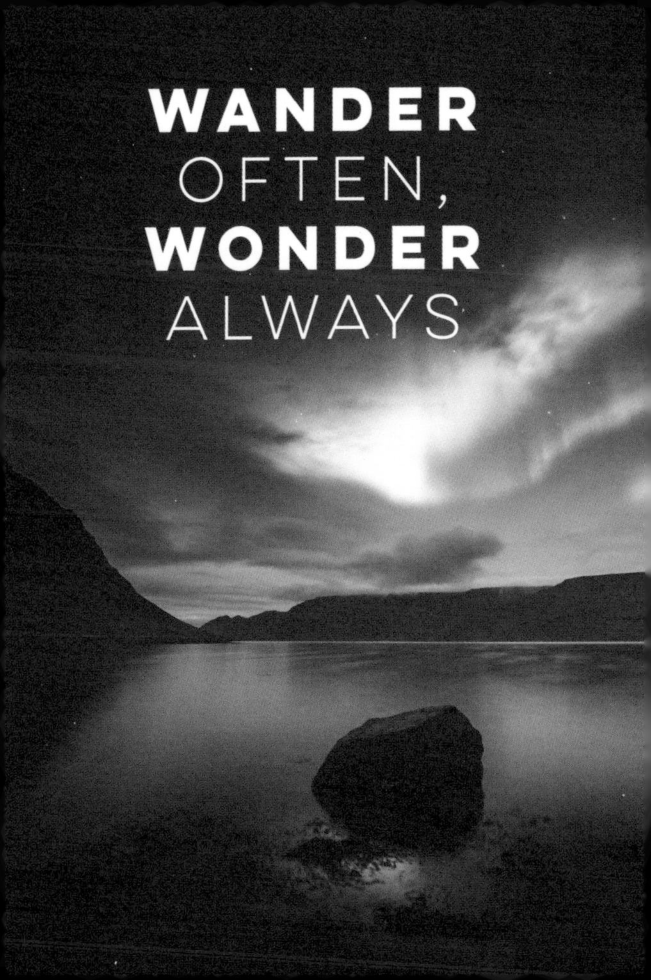
WANDER
OFTEN,
WONDER
ALWAYS

THE

CLEAREST WAY
INTO THE
UNIVERSE

IS THROUGH
A FOREST
WILDERNESS.

JOHN MUIR

BEWARE; FOR I AM FEARLESS, AND THEREFORE POWERFUL.

Mary Shelley

NO ATTAINMENT IS
BEYOND HIS REACH
WHO EQUIPS HIMSELF WITH
PATIENCE
TO ACHIEVE IT.

Jean de La Bruyère

WE SHOULD
COME HOME FROM...
ADVENTURES AND
PERILS AND
DISCOVERIES EVERY
DAY, WITH NEW
EXPERIENCE AND
CHARACTER.

HENRY DAVID THOREAU

ADVENTURE IS NOT OUTSIDE MAN; IT IS WITHIN.

George Eliot

THERE IS NO

greater joy

THAN TO HAVE AN

endlessly

CHANGING HORIZON.

CHRISTOPHER McCANDLESS

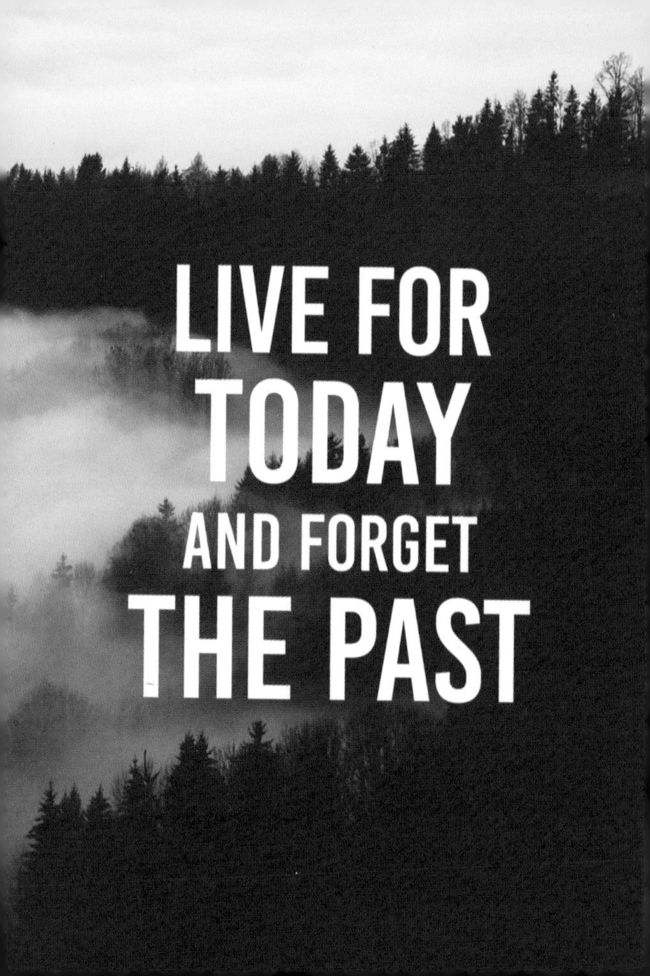
LIVE FOR
TODAY
AND FORGET
THE PAST

YOU'VE GOT TO GET UP EVERY MORNING WITH DETERMINATION IF YOU'RE GOING TO GO TO BED WITH SATISFACTION.

George Lorimer

Adventure

FINDS THOSE WHO...
GO OUT AND

➤➤➤————————➤

GET IT!

NOT ALL THOSE WHO

wander

ARE LOST.

J. R. R. TOLKIEN

SO THROW OFF
THE BOWLINES.
SAIL AWAY
FROM THE SAFE
HARBOUR.
CATCH THE
TRADE WINDS
IN YOUR SAILS.
EXPLORE.
DREAM.
DISCOVER.

Sarah Frances Brown

IMAGE CREDITS

IF YOU'RE INTERESTED IN FINDING OUT MORE ABOUT OUR BOOKS, FIND US ON FACEBOOK AT SUMMERSDALE PUBLISHERS AND FOLLOW US ON TWITTER AT @SUMMERSDALE.

WWW.SUMMERSDALE.COM